Cries of a Broken Heart

The hidden words we don't always share.

This book may not be reproduced in any way without written consent from the author.

Copyright ©2024 MakenzieRaeBooks

All rights reserved.

To my reader,

There was a time when I thought silence would save me. That if I buried the ache deep enough, no one would see the wreckage inside.

But pain has a voice. Even when whispered, it echoes.

*This book is not just a collection of poems.
It's a timeline of survival. A record of every moment I felt forgotten, discarded, or unlovable — and still got up the next morning anyway.*

The first version of Cries of a Broken Heart was written from within the rubble. This version is me sorting through it — finding the sharpest shards, holding them up to the light, and saying: "Here. This hurt me. But I'm still here."

*I've added new poems that bled out of me quietly.
I've organized the collection into pieces of a story:
the fall, the silence, the memories, and what comes after.*

If you're holding this, I hope you see your own heartbreak somewhere in these pages. And I hope you feel a little less alone inside it.

Let's cry together for a while. Then keep going.

—Makenzie Rae

*Dedicate to the one still pretending you're fine—
this book was written with you in mind.*

These are the cries I tried to hide. But now I let them echo so y'all know you're not alone.

Cries of a Broken Heart 1

THE FALL 1

- No More 3
- A Tempest Calling 5
- Nothing Left 6
- Pointless 9
- Sweet Untruth 11
- Rinse and Repeat 13
- I Miss You 15
- I Hate You 17
- Locked 19
- Weeping Willow 21
- The Craving 23
- I Quit 25
- Thirsty 27
- Lies 29
- You Lie 30
- Like the Wind 33
- You Win 34
- Waiting 37
- Imaginary Storm 39
- Fairytale Dreams 41
- Tough Conversations 43
- Exceptions to the Rule 45
- Love Defined 46
- My Made-Up Life 49
- SAD 51
- Losing Battle 53
- Unwanted Rubbish 55
- Slivers of Hope 57
- Echoes in the Abyss 59
- Unchosen 61
- Drifting Away 65

This Time, Again 67
THE SILENCE THAT SCREAMS 69
Lost at Sea 71
Explosion 73
Except 75
Reality 77
Island Life 79
Depths of Despair 81
Winter 83
Living With Lies 85
Hide 87
Come A Little Closer 89
Titanium Heart 91
Infestation 93
Ice Queen 95
Devastated 97
I Smile 98
Inside 101
Broken 103
Suffocating 105
Questions 107
Teetering 109
A Tempest Raging 111
Treading Water 113
But 114
Deeper 117
Dare 119
It's Complicated 121
Voices 122
Breaking Point 125
The Battle 127
The Craving 129
Whiplash 131
Silent Death 133
Her Diary 135

THE WEIGHT OF REMEMBERING 137

- Fool's Anonymous 139
- Cloak and Dagger 141
- Too Many Questions 143
- Self-Betrayal 145
- The Battle Within 147
- Insensible 149
- Unreality 151
- Never Wake Up 153
- Two-Faced 155
- Numb 157
- City of Lies 159
- Addiction 161
- Hope 162
- Buried 165
- I'm Sorry 166
- Too Much to Ask For 169
- By Any Other Name 170
- Battle 173
- One Coin, Two Faces 174
- Too Broken 177
- Strangers 179
- Monstrous Desires 183
- New Normal 184
- Good Enough 189
- A Show 190
- Wait 193
- Remember 195
- I'm Great 196
- Relentless Heart 199
- The Monster Inside 201
- Still She Sits 202
- Masked Woman 205
- Bleeding Hands 206
- Ghost of a Life Past 209

    Always the Fool.. 210
    Façade.. 212
    Hold On 214
IF I WAKE TOMORROW 217
    A Pheonix Rising 218
    The Little Things 221
    Her Decision 222
    Growing Pains... 225
    This Day 229
    Once Upon a Lie 230
    Unexpected.. 232
    Just for a Moment 235
AUTHOR'S NOTE 237

THE FALL

The heart doesn't shatter like glass.
It rots in silence.
And when it's no longer useful,
it is thrown out with yesterday's trash.

THE FALL

No More

I needed you today
I had a moment's lapse of vulnerability
I needed to know that no matter what, you'd be there for me
No grumbling, no complaining
That it wasn't an inconvenience
That *I'm* not an inconvenience
I didn't ask for anything big, just a simple favor
I trusted you with my vulnerability, my heart, me
I'm sorry
I didn't know it was such a major issue
Such an overwhelming weight for you
I didn't mean to be such a nuisance
But don't worry, I'm stronger now
I won't ask for help
I won't ask for comfort
I won't ask for you

THE FALL

A Tempest Calling

I dip my toe in to test the waters
It's cold and murky and I don't trust it
Still, I take a leap of faith and step in
Its frigid iciness threatens to steal my breath
I want to turn back but every wave whispers
"You can trust me"

Wanting it to be true, I continue walking
Every step a struggle not to lose myself
Waist high, the water coaxes me to go further
I struggle to stand, but I keep going
Just as it reaches my head, it turns
No longer is it calm and inviting

It rushes and crashes and drags me under
Wrestling to maintain my bearings, I fight back
I pull and push to return to safe ground
I'm nearly drowned beneath the torrent of lies
Slowly I drag my bedraggled body ashore
Fighting to stand, I turn to the water and whisper
"I can't trust you"

Nothing Left

Walking around with a smile on my face
But a broken heart inside
You promised to love me forever
But apparently you lied

Time and time again I told you what I want
I told you what I need
I didn't think they were excessive requests
To be heard, to be held, to be seen

But it seems my requests fell upon deaf ears
That you didn't hear a word
Instead, you did what you wanted to do
And left me here to burn

Burn with feelings of doubt and betrayal
Of never being enough
Wishing my love could satisfy you
And we could get out of this rut

I tried to be what you needed me to be
To keep you from going astray
But what I offered just wasn't enough
For you still went your own way

What else could I have done or said
But let you play your games
And hope that when you came back home
It wouldn't be the same

That I would be all you wanted in life
That you would choose to stay with me
Instead of stepping out with someone else
And leaving me here to bleed

This repeated pattern in our lives
Has definitely taken its toll
It's taken everything from inside me
My life, my heart, my soul

THE FALL

THE FALL

Pointless

Empty
Hollow
Words spoken

    Void
    Barren
    Promises made

  Vain
  Valueless
  Trusting over and over again

      Futile
      Senseless
      Hope that they'll be kept

THE FALL

Sweet Untruth

Walls, fences, barricades
Taken down by a promise
Slowly and painstakingly disassembled

    The thawing of a heart
    Chipping away the hardness
    Nurtured to life by expressions of love

Steel, impenetrable, solid
The rebuilding of a wall
Quickly reassembled by unfaithfulness

    A frozen heart
    Becoming like titanium
    No longer beating inside the chest

Love and faithfulness
Lying for peace of mind
Killing everyone in its grasp

THE FALL

Rinse and Repeat

Over
And over
And over
And over
Again
        You make a promise
        I foolishly believe
        You break your promise
           I hurt
           I cry
                You make a promise
                I foolishly believe
                You break your promise
                    Rinse and repeat

Over
And over
And over
And over
Again
        You make a promise
        I foolishly believe
        You break your promise
           I hurt
           I cry
           I die a little more
                You make a promise
                I foolishly believe
                You break your promise
                    Rinse and repeat

THE FALL

I Miss You

I miss you.
I miss the way you held me close when I was falling apart.
I miss how you gave me strength when I was weak.
I miss the safety I found in the arms that were only for me.
I miss the promises you made and the way you kept them.
I miss how you wanted to know everything about me and my passions.
I miss the encouragement you gave me to step out and chase my dreams.
I miss so much about you, but mostly:
I miss the person you said you'd be,
but never was.

THE FALL

I Hate You

I hate you for saying you love me,
then bringing about more heartache.

I hate you for drying the old tears from my eyes,
only to cause an ocean's worth of new ones.

I hate you for making me feel special,
then turning around and making me feel
worthless.

I hate you for making me trust you enough to
start lowering my wall,
just for you to cause me to reinforce it.

I hate you for promising me one thing,
but doing the other.

I hate you for making me fall in love with you,
only to have you break my heart.

THE FALL

Locked

I look at you and instead of seeing love,
I see lies
Every time you speak,
I hear emptiness
The promises you make slip through my hands
like sand
Too numerous to count
Too inconsequential to hold
You understand, you'll try, you'll do
But you don't
You never do
Things will get better, be better
But they're not
The same lies I used to cling to, now just roll
right off
There is no space inside for even a little trust to
seep through
My heart is locked up like a vault
You can't access it
You no longer have the key

20

THE FALL

Weeping Willow

Weeping willow hear me cry,
Weeping willow see me sigh.
For the only one that I have loved
Has left me for another one.

Weeping willow smell the air,
Weeping willow, it isn't fair.
He shot my heart with Cupid's arrow,
Then let it loose like a flying sparrow.

Weeping willow feel my pain,
Weeping willow feel the same.
Comfort me in these weary days
When I need you most in many ways.

Weeping willow look about,
Weeping willow see the doubt.
The doubt that lies within my head;
The doubt that cries for help instead.

Weeping willow touch my heart
Weeping willow, it fell apart.
It does hurt but now I see
That our love just cannot be.

THE FALL

The Craving

It's an addiction
I can't go without it
I've tried
But not very hard
I just don't want to
It's intoxicating
I crave it like oxygen
It fills my soul
Quenches the desire in my heart
Brings a smile to my face
A twinkle in my eye
I yearn for it every day
My life seems darker when I don't have it
It woke me up
Made me hope again
Believe in more
It has become the food I need to survive
The meal I crave over and over again
The one I'll never grow tired of

THE FALL

I Quit

I quit
I surrender
Resignation submitted
No longer am I living with the false promises
Erroneous vows uttered in sheer desperation

I refuse to accept these useless proclamations
These fabricated declarations of hope, of change
Empty statements of transformation
Counterfeit truths
Lip service

THE FALL

Thirsty

I went to the well of our love to fetch some water
I was parched and desired its sweet relief
Lowering the basket, I waited in hopeful anticipation
I just knew that the water from our well would satisfy my thirsting heart
I was weak with fatigue from the trek up the mountain to reach it
Slowly and painfully, I turned the handle to crank up the basket
I reached in to cup its life-giving supply only to cry out in despair
No longer could it offer support to sustain my life
No longer could I bask in its wonderous beauty, shimmering deep within the earth
For I found that our well was no longer a living, bubbling stream
The water was gone, and the bucket was dry

THE FALL

Lies

You can trust me.
I'm changing.
I'm not going to hurt you.
You don't need to worry.
I'm not going to lie to you.
I'm not the same person.
I won't let you down.
I promise.
You can trust me.
The lies they say.
The lies we believe.

You Lie

You say you love me
You say you're sorry and that you want to be with me forever
You promise to do better, be better
You lie

How many times do I have to hear you spout your untruths
Why do you continue to offer your false securities
This time it will be different
This time you'll listen
This time you'll be what I need you to be
This time...
Never comes

I don't know how much longer I can cling to the ever-weakening branches of one day
One day you'll stop
One day you'll hear
One day you'll see that the heart which once raced so wildly with love barely has the strength to beat
That it's weak from being shattered and pieced

together too many times
That I can't keep living like this

I can't keep holding on to broken promises
I can't keep hoping that it will get better
It will kill me
I'm already almost dead

THE FALL

Like the Wind

Your words are like the wind, breathing new life into me
Filling me up, resurrecting my hope

Your words are like the wind, sweeping inside my soul
Sifting the strands of doubt, blowing away my fallen dreams

Your words are like the wind, rushing through my heart
Scattering the broken pieces, leaving nothing behind

Your words are like the wind, sweeping lies to and fro
Shouting deceitful exclamations, whispering vain promises

Your words are like the wind, fabricated, wispy
Empty

You Win

Congratulations
You win
I hope you are happy with your prize
You did it
You finally broke me
The heart that was so carefully pieced together is shattered
I tried protecting it and only opening it when you could be trusted with it
Apparently I opened it too soon
I handed you my heart along with the hammer that you used on it
I will not be able to find the million shards that it busted in to
I will just have to piece it back together with the splinters I can find
And if it ends up being smaller than it was before, then maybe it'll be a little safer
A smaller target to hit and break
A smaller room for you to try squeezing in to
Today I will rebuild my heart and reinforce it will steel
I will make it even harder to let another in to break it
I will hide it away so it cannot be smashed again, lest it be gone forever

Today I lose the ability to open my heart again
But hey, congratulations
You did it

THE FALL

THE FALL

Waiting

"I'm going to change."
"I'm going to do better."
"I'm going to be better."
I keep waiting.
    "I won't talk like that anymore."
    "I won't act like that anymore."
    "I won't be like that anymore."
    I keep waiting.
"I'll get help."
"I'll try harder."
"I'll see someone."
I keep waiting.
    "I'll be your rock."
    "I'll be your support."
    "I'll be your iron."
    I keep waiting.
"I will..."
"As soon as..."
"When..."
I'm done waiting.

THE FALL

Imaginary Storm

Caught up
Swirling round and round
Out of control
Feet swept off the ground

    Carrying away
    With reckless abandon
    Words long to be freed
    Thoughts left undone

        Turmoil inside
        A deep, yearning desire
        To step out of the water
        And into the fire

           Burning bridges
           Destroyed by the flame
           A hope that can't be
           Worlds forever changed

                A reality to undo
                A touch to dream of
                A reckless abandon
                An imaginary love

THE FALL

Fairytale Dreams

She used to dream that she would have a
fairytale type of love
The kind that would stand the test of time and
trials
One where she was free to be herself
Free to be vulnerable and open about her
worries and her hopes
That she would be supported and encouraged
to chase her dreams
She used to dream that she would find a man
who would be strong enough to carry her
To pick her up when she was down
A man who would know how she needed to be
loved and would do it
Who would not have to be told over and over
again exactly how to love her
She used to dream that she would be
everything her true love ever wanted
That he would only have eyes for her
That he couldn't fathom the thought of being
with another
And that he would love her in a way that left no
doubt of the depths of his love
That he wouldn't want anyone or anything else
She used to dream

THE FALL

Tough Conversations

It's time to come back to reality
Get your head out of the clouds
You've lived in your land of delusion long enough
Truth is truth and life is life
It cannot be imagined or made-up
No more pretending, or wishing, or wanting
Only what's real, what you know
Stop letting your heart run off in the fairytale it created
Get it under control
You know what the truth is
Don't let your heart try to mix you up with its unrealistic desires
Use your brain to guide you, not your heart
It is not trustworthy
It lives in a world where impossible things become possible
But you know better
It's time to start acting like it

THE FALL

Exceptions to the Rule

You're enough, all I could ever want.
Except for the others I want, they don't count.

There's nothing I wouldn't do for you.
Except love you the way you need to be loved.

I'm here for you; you're not a burden.
Except when you ask me to do something that inconveniences me.

I love you the way you are; don't change.
Except when it allows me to do what I want to do.

You deserve to be happy and loved.
Except when I choose to make you sad.

You belong with me, and I belong with you.
Except when I want to try new things.

You deserve nothing but the whole truth.
Except when it's something I don't want you to know.

You should expect promises to be kept.
Except for the ones I make, they don't count.

Love Defined

She knows he loves her, or does she?
He's there for her, or is he?
What does it mean to love someone?
If it means being physically there, then yes, he loves her.
If it means making pretty promises of change then backing out just to make them again, then yes, he loves her.
If it means only giving enough to make her feel a little bit loved, then yes, he loves her.
She can stand on those truths.
She can try to.
But what if it's more than that?
What if loving someone is putting them first?
Showing them love in the ways they receive it.
Holding them in your arms just because you want to be close to them.
Taking their hand and leading the way.
Listening and caring about what they are saying.
Making a promise, and keeping it.
Building them up in words and actions.
Supporting and encouraging their dreams.
Pushing them to be better than the day before.
Being the rock they can lean on.

That they can depend on.
That doesn't do things to destroy trust.
Telling her and showing her every day that she is enough.
That no matter what, he will be there in every way she needs him to be.
That he will never betray her.
Hurt her.
Break her.
Then she would know that he loves her, his actions would have told her so.

THE FALL

My Made-Up Life

I'm in love with a dream
A made-up figment of my imagination
A cruel beast of what-ifs inside my own head
A touch, yet I feel more
A look, yet I see a promise
A word, yet I hear a loving whisper
What is real, yet what I foolishly hope for
I need to get my mind and heart under control
They are running away in their fantasies
Making up fairytales and trying to get me to believe them
They aren't real, I know that, yet I wish they were
At the same time, I don't
Nothing could come of them, no matter how I would want otherwise
I'm locked in a mental and emotional cage of my own creation

THE FALL

SAD

Swirling emotions
Spinning round and round
Slowly pulling me deeper

Away from hope
Absent from peace
Aggravating my mind

Dragging me away
Digging its talons in
Destroying my soul

THE FALL

Losing Battle

Mystical
Fantasy
Imaginary
I see things that aren't there
They don't exist
An alternate reality
A break in time
A psychotic break
I dream of a love made in my mind
It's not real
Wishful thinking
Mistaken belief
Self-deception
I feel the fantom touch of more
It's not true
Clinging
Persistent
Entrenched
I fight the feelings I stupidly desire
I'm not winning

THE FALL

Unwanted Rubbish

I live in a life full of unreality
One made up completely by me

A world where there will always an us
A life so simply sweet that it makes fairytales envious

Where impossible dreams come to pass
And I don't have to live in the aftermath

No broken hearts, no empty promises, no lies
No tears overflowing like waterfalls from my eyes

But no matter how hard I wish it could be
These machinations aren't my reality

I keep getting overwhelmed by these imaginings that are not true
And I have to accept, again, that there is no me and you

Because although my made-up world is perfect in every way
I always wake up and remember that I was thrown away

Tossed into the bin in a broken heap
I am the picked over waste that

THE FALL

Slivers of Hope

I'm dead
There's nothing left
Everything in me is sliced to pieces
Killed from the inside out
Destroyed by the slivers of hope that I've
swallowed
Believed in
Hoped for
Little by little
Time after time
It cut through the barriers that were meant to
keep me safe
Split open my lungs
Drowning me
Shredded what was left of my heart
It no longer beats

THE FALL

Echoes in the Abyss

I'm drowning in the deep abyss
I don't want to be here
I search for a way out but only see murky darkness
No means of escape
I dream of a better time
A better life
A life filled with love
Where I am important
Worthy enough to be kept
To be held forever
To be chosen
But that is only my imagination
There is no light of love
Only bleak emptiness

THE FALL

Unchosen

She wants to go
To leave the pain behind
But she's afraid to move
'Cause what if she will never find

Someone to be a rock
She can lean on when she feels weak
A heartbeat of light
When her world seems so bleak

Someone with a shoulder strong enough
To fight off all her fears
Yet gentle enough
To wipe away the smallest of tears

She's been alone for so long
Having to fend for herself
Would she even know
How to depend on somebody else

Sticking to all she's ever known
Feels like her safest bet
Because she doesn't know
If she could even let

Someone be her strength
To wholeheartedly depend on
Could she trust him completely
After everything that's been done

To her throughout her life
From those who claimed they loved her
They lied and abused and broke her heart
Shattering it forever

She picked up the pieces
To assemble her heart again
And waited for the deluge
Of hurtful lies to begin

She doesn't believe there is a man
Who would take her battered heart
Wipe it off, repair the cracks
Help her give love a brand-new start

She's afraid that pain and deceit
Is all she'll ever know of love
Because man after man
Has proven to her that instead of

A knight in shining armor
Ready fight and defend
She was only worthy of
A life of pretend

Pretend words, pretend love
Pretend promises, pretend life
They say the right words
But their actions are a knife

That carve out her heart
One piece at a time
She uses the last of her strength
To try and climb

Out of the dark abyss
That has become her reality
And start the day again
In this world of her normality

She has to smile through tears
That no longer fall
And not let others know
That she's ready to give up on it all

THE FALL

THE FALL

Drifting Away

Dreaming with my eyes wide shut
I look to a future I do not see
Living the tragedy of peace of mind
I place hope in a lie I do not believe

Fading into a deepening abyss
I drift further from the life I wish I had
Suffocating on the stench of betrayal
I breathe the toxic air of a love gone bad

Clinging to the remnants of a heart destroyed
I loosen my grip with each need unheard
Dying each day from the inside out
I slip closer to oblivion with every broken word

THE FALL

This Time, Again

I'm sorry I hurt you again.
I know I said before that I wouldn't do it
again... again.
But this time, again, I really mean it.
I'm, again, choosing us, choosing you.
Again, you are all I want.
Again, can we start again?
I will show you that I mean it this time.
This time, I will not break my promise...
again.
I will stand by my word this time.
I know you've heard it all before, but this time
is different... again.
It is not the same "again" as last time.
This time, I really, really mean it... again.

THE SILENCE THAT SCREAMS

THE SILENCE THAT SCREAMS

*Not all deaths are loud.
Some come slowly—
One unspoken feeling at a time.*

THE SILENCE THAT SCREAMS

Lost at Sea

Relentless waves crash onto the shores of my broken heart
Sweeping out to sea the hopes and dreams it once held
Its overpowering salt burning the open wounds of my shattered life
Oh, that I could run far enough to escape its raging torrent
Instead, I am left to swim in the dark murky depths, held captive by its lies
Its offering of peace, of freedom, of love
I drown a little more everyday as the icy water breaks down the barricades meant to protect me
They weigh me down, dragging me further into the very thing I wish to be free of
Taking me deeper and deeper until I can no longer see the light, the way out
I am dying

THE SILENCE THAT SCREAMS

Explosion

I hold my breath and wait
Wait for the pain and the anger and the sorrow
and the disappointment to pass
It doesn't
Instead, it pounds inside my mind
Pushing and pushing and pushing
Pulsing and throbbing
Trying to escape the box it has been buried in
I close my eyes and hope that it doesn't kill me
I try to shove it back down into its prison cell
It resists
It's tired of being ignored
It wants to be free
It wants to explode and destroy everything in its path
I try to fight it, but I'm losing strength.

THE SILENCE THAT SCREAMS

Except

I'm bold, I'm strong, I'm indestructible
>   Except when I'm not

I can fight, I can overcome, I can be invincible
>   Except when I can't

I have power, I have peace, I have hope
>   Except when I don't

I don't need to be helped, I don't need to be held, I don't need to feel loved
>   Except when I do

I could pretend, I could give up, I could walk away
>   Except that I won't

THE SILENCE THAT SCREAMS

Reality

So many questions batter my mind
Never giving me a moment's peace
Round and round they chase each other
Jumping from one answer to another
Do this, do that, ignore this, think about that
They won't stop
I just want to curl into a ball
Seal a cocoon around myself
Not let anyone or any thought in
I'd be free
I wouldn't have to pretend anymore
Smile when I'm dying inside
I could block it all out
I could be at peace
But the reality is I can't
I have to live, keep going, day to day
I have to face the fact that I'm messed up inside
That my mind says one thing and my heart another
I have to face the questions I want to hide from
And hope they don't utterly destroy me

THE SILENCE THAT SCREAMS

Island Life

Mask the pain
Ignore the hurt
Hide the shame
You are strong enough
You don't need anyone
You can walk alone
People lie
They destroy
Don't let them in
Don't trust them
Swallow the bitter pill of emptiness
Let it numb your entire being
Heart and mind blocked
No pain
No heartache
No shame
You can't feel anything
You *won't* feel anything
You refuse to

THE SILENCE THAT SCREAMS

Depths of Despair

I look up through the cold, murky water
I see the light slipping through
I can almost feel the warmth it promises
It lies
Its false promises lure me into an imagined peace
It draws me closer, making me think I'm safe
I open my mouth to breathe in the fresh, lifesaving air
Instead, I choke on the pungent water that keeps me captive
It drags me into its frigid depths, draining the life from me
I fight against its pull, struggling to reach the light
Its grip is too strong to break
I don't think I can go on
I'm dying

THE SILENCE THAT SCREAMS

Winter

I wait in solitude for the changing of the season
The cold has staked its claim and taken over everything
The icy wind blows away the last vestiges of my shattered heart
The heart that once was full of hope for the future
I lie down and surrender to the frigid emptiness
I wait with broken promises clutched tightly in my frozen hand
I die a little more waiting for them to bring forth a warmer time

THE SILENCE THAT SCREAMS

Living With Lies

You look, but don't see
What you do see, isn't
You hope for more
And pray for less
You want a truth
Yet live a lie
Do you even know what you're doing
What you're thinking
What you truly desire
Too afraid to ask
Too ashamed to tell
You're dying inside
But outwardly smiling
Don't let them see
They will hate you
Be strong
Push through
This too will pass
Eventually

THE SILENCE THAT SCREAMS

Hide

Hide
Don't let them see
Keep it inside
Push it down
Bury it beneath your smile
Pretend you're not hurting
That the pain isn't suffocating you
Perform
Act as if everything is fine
It's good
No problems here
Trick them into believing you
That you're not broken inside
You're not hollow
That you're heart hasn't been shattered
The shards scattered
Never to be put together again
It's too hard
It's too late
It's too destroyed

THE SILENCE THAT SCREAMS

Come A Little Closer

Come a little closer and feel my fading life.
Feel the empty nothingness, feel the pain I hide.

Come a little closer and see the tears that fill my eyes.
See the heart that's bleeding, see the blood that never dries.

Come a little closer and smell the stench that's on my skin.
Smell the fear I radiate, smell the fright that's stuck within.

Come a little closer and taste my broken lips.
Taste the dehydration, taste the cuts and splits.

Come a little closer and listen to me cry.
Listen to me hurting, listen to me die.

THE SILENCE THAT SCREAMS

Titanium Heart

Titanium
Unbreakable
Impenetrable
Some people say that they have a wall around their heart
But I say that there is no wall around my heart
For a wall can be scaled
It can be knocked down
It can be destroyed
No, there is no wall
Instead, my heart is trapped inside a titanium ball
No ending, no beginning
No way for someone to get in
No way for it to be broken
I keep my heart protected inside my ball
I don't worry that my heart will be trampled on
That it will be abused and misused
Nobody can get inside my titanium heart
But neither can I get out
I am trapped in here with all the pain of the past
With everything that happened to my heart
before I forged this ball of protection
I cannot outrun my hurt
I cannot escape my shame
Nobody can hurt me
Nobody can help me

THE SILENCE THAT SCREAMS

Infestation

Please help
I'm choking
I can't breathe
Anger and pain clogs my throat
The need to scream so thick it blocks any air from coming in
I'm suffocating on the words that cannot escape
I swallow them down along with the whispered promises that are never kept
I can't digest the lies that I've been fed over and over again
They infest my intestines, refusing to be processed out
They have made a nest inside of me and are taking over
My heart is not my own anymore
It has been taken captive by false promises and empty words
I fear that it has lost the will to survive
That it has given up all hope
That it is barely clinging to life
That it is already dead

THE SILENCE THAT SCREAMS

Ice Queen

Frozen
I breathe out the frost that has infiltrated my veins
Declared war on my mind
And overtaken my heart
Tears can no longer fall
They have become daggers, piercing me from within
No amount of warmth can thaw me
The cold has completely taken control
It has transformed me
Created a new creature
Made me an ice queen

THE SILENCE THAT SCREAMS

Devastated

How many times can a heart shatter before it can no longer be patched back together?

How long before all that remains are the fantom pains where the heart once was?

How many times can trust be destroyed before it comes back to destroy me?

How long before I am blown away like the ashes that used to be my heart?

How many times can I pick myself up, tape me back together, and trust again?

How long before it utterly annihilates any semblance of who I am, who I used to be?

I Smile

When hard times hit, I smile
When life doesn't seem right, I smile
When I can't make sense of the world around me, I smile
When all I want to do is cry, I smile
When I'm at my breaking point, I smile
When the pressure builds and builds, I smile
When I hold back the words that are determined to burst out, I smile
When it feels like my heart is breaking into a billion tiny shards, I smile
When I'm empty and broken inside, I smile
To keep the peace, I smile
To keep the darkness at bay, I smile
To prevent anything or anyone from getting close enough to hurt me, I smile
To prevent the tears from flooding my life, I smile
To prevent anyone from seeing that I am dying inside, I smile
To keep the wall around my heart securely in place, I smile
To prove to the world that I'm OK, I smile
To lie to the person staring back at me from the mirror, I smile

To not have a complete and total breakdown, I smile
To hold my life and myself together, I smile
To survive, I smile

THE SILENCE THAT SCREAMS

Inside

I lay on my side
So that I can hide
The anguish I buried inside

The heartache and pain
The guilt and shame
Self-loathing and self-blame

I try to be strong
Say nothing is wrong
But the battle's too long

Oh that I could run
And bask in the sun
Undo what's been done

Words left unsaid
Stay stuck in my head
Leaving me for dead

THE SILENCE THAT SCREAMS

Broken

Once believed
Once sought after
Once a dream
Once was love

    Now is sorrow
    Now is blame
    Now is fighting
    Now is hiding

Full of pain
Full of wishing
Full of untruths
Full of trying

    Broken pieces
    Broken promises
    Broken hearts
    Broken reality

Built up protection
Built up defense
Built up separation
Built up walls

    No more trusting
    No more believing
    No more hoping
    No more love

THE SILENCE THAT SCREAMS

Suffocating

Suffocating
I can't breathe
I'm drowning in the tears I refuse to shed
The tears that keep my fortress firmly secure
I can't let them escape
I can't let them win
I won't let them destroy me
Again
I will hold them in
Overflowing the well buried deep inside
Filling up every space
Stealing the oxygen from my lungs
Flooding my heart and stopping its beat
Killing me
One teardrop at a time
Dying

THE SILENCE THAT SCREAMS

Questions

What do you say when the words won't come?

When you don't have the strength to even whisper that you are too tired to fight anymore?

That it is taking every ounce of your energy just to breathe through the pain?

Do you keep sludging through, hoping that it gets better?

Praying the next day will be the day that the heartache releases its grip on your lungs?

That you can actually begin to let down your guard?

That you can open your heart without fear of it being trampled on again?

Or do you put on your happy face and pretend like everything is OK?

That you're not slowly dying inside?

That you don't wake up every morning fighting to be positive?

If so, how long can you live like that?

Are you even truly alive?

THE SILENCE THAT SCREAMS

Teetering

I'm teetering on the precipice of this ever-growing mountain
The chasm separating us growing wider with every breath
I want to reach out, but I'm too afraid of falling
Afraid that if I take the leap to reach you, I'll be let go of again

THE SILENCE THAT SCREAMS

A Tempest Raging

I'm sinking in the vast ocean that is my mind
Thought after thought swirling round and round
The never-ending vortex spinning wildly out of control
It's choking the life out of me
Suffocating the very essence of my being
I try to swim against its raging flow, but I am losing strength
Should I surrender to its tirade
Let go and see where the cyclone takes me
Or should I ignore the water filling up my lungs, stealing my breath
Pretend it's not there, not real, and just go on living a lie

THE SILENCE THAT SCREAMS

Treading Water

I sink
I gasp
Air rushes in
I push to the top
I kick
I fight
I battle the storm
Struggle to keep my head above the waves
Try not to let it take me under
Grip me in its ruthless talons
I push
I fight
I keep going

But

Today I just want to break down
I want to shed the tears that have been dammed up for so long
Break the barrier that I spent a lifetime constructing
I want to scream as loud as I can to feel a sense of release
But I can't

My mind won't let the wall it has used its logic to fabricate come down
Sometimes I think that if I could bang my head against a wall, it would shatter
I don't want to hurt myself, just relieve some pressure
To shake out the thoughts that invade my mind
I don't want to need anyone
I don't want to crave someone's touch
But I do

I want to curl into a ball and be rocked like a baby
To be held and taken care of
I want to feel love's arms wrap around me and hold me tight

I want to feel its sweet caress reassuring me
Each touch whispering that I am cared for
That I am safe
That I can let go
But these things won't happen
They are the made-up dreams of a heart that once believed it was protected

THE SILENCE THAT SCREAMS

Deeper

It's all good
Things will work out
It's normal
But it's not
It's deeper than I let on
I only show the surface level
What people would expect to see
I don't tell them of the hidden secrets buried deep inside
The truths that only I can know
I dare not tell them
They wouldn't understand
I don't even understand
The why's and how's of it all
The what would be's or could be's
The if only's and what ifs
The why would you's
And the how could you's
How can I tell them, when I have a hard enough time telling myself

THE SILENCE THAT SCREAMS

Dare

To know or not to know
To feel or to be numb
To hope or to ignore
To forsake or to love

Ask for the answer
Or let secrets be kept
Hope against hope
A heart will be met

I do and I don't
I want to but I can't
Act on the thoughts
Or keep them in hand

A dare yet not daring
Foolish in hoping
I swallow down words
Best left unspoken

THE SILENCE THAT SCREAMS

It's Complicated

"How are you doing?"
A simple question that I can't really answer
"I'm fine. I'm great."
It's the response I'll give
But I'm lying
The truth is I don't really know
I don't know how I'm doing
How I'm feeling
I'm good and bad all at once
Happy but sad
I'm filled with joy
But also, broken and empty
Daring, yet afraid
Smart and stupid
Determined but still conflicted
So how am I supposed to answer
Tell them everything I'm thinking?
People don't want the truth
They want to hear that everything's great
Couldn't be better
Even when it's not

Voices

What do I do with the voices in my head?
How do I ignore their ever-present barrage?
Do this. Don't do that. It's ok. It really ain't.
Constantly repeating their montage.

Want what you can't have.
Hate what you do.
Embrace the unknown.
Just make a move.

Fight the emotions.
They aren't right.
Bottle up the feelings.
Pack them away tight.

You can't fight this.
You must fight that.
Smile through plain.
Don't let them see you react.

Push people away
You just need a hug.
You don't need anyone.
You only want to be loved.

It's real. It's not.
They're good. They're bad.
It's up. It's down.
You're happy. You're sad.

My mind is spinning with too many words.
All of them fighting to take control.
It's causing chaos and confusion within.
Stealing my peace and leaving a big hole.

THE SILENCE THAT SCREAMS

Breaking Point

Break free
    Release it
        Let it go
            It's okay
                Relax
                    Don't hold it in
                Breathe
            Push it out
        Escape
      Move on
Impossible

THE SILENCE THAT SCREAMS

The Battle

I can see a light trying to break through the darkness that has shrouded my life.

The insecurity, the doubt, and the shame that threatens to destroy me every day.

I strain to keep my eyes focused on the light so that it doesn't completely disappear.

Taking with it the last bit of hope that my heart struggles to cling to.

I pray that I'll have the strength to keep my eyes from straying from the light.

That I don't surrender to the darkness before the light can utterly defeat it.

THE SILENCE THAT SCREAMS

The Craving

It's an addiction
I can't go without it
I've tried
But not very hard
I just don't want to
It's intoxicating
I crave it like oxygen
It fills my soul
Quenches the desire in my heart
Brings a smile to my face
A twinkle in my eye
I yearn for it every day
My life seems darker when I don't have it
It woke me up
Made me hope again
Believe in more
It has become the food I need to survive
The meal I crave over and over again
The one I'll never grow tired of

THE SILENCE THAT SCREAMS

Whiplash

Life is a yo-yo
Some days you've accepted that things are the way they are
You're not sad about it
It is what it is
Then other days you're sitting there and out of nowhere, you're down
You hate that things are the way they are
You want the days back where things were easy, good even
You want to cry over a life lost
Then, BOOM! You're up again
You're ok with the way things are, content even
Up and down, up and down
Over and over again
It's exhausting

THE SILENCE THAT SCREAMS

Silent Death

I feel too much
All at once
Every emotion battling for control
Overwhelming me
Rage and sorrow
Hope and fear
Agony and relief
All fighting inside of me
Turning my brain to mush
Destroying me little by little
Scream
Let it out
Release the pressure
But I can't
My lips are frozen
They refuse to open
To yield to my command
They've felt the sting of unspoken words
Tasted the bitterness of tears shed in vain
They are rebelling against me
Thinking they are protecting me
They're not
They are fortifying their barricades
Causing the pressure to build
My feelings piling on top of each other
Clogging my throat
The silence of lips that once protected me is now killing me

THE SILENCE THAT SCREAMS

Her Diary

He said he loved her.
He said she was all he ever wanted.
He lied.
Proving to her already damaged heart
that it really wasn't worthy
of being loved,
and held,
and protected,
by the man who said he loved her.
Who promised to be there for her,
only to change his mind.

THE SILENCE THAT SCREAMS

THE WEIGHT OF REMEMBERING

Some ghosts don't haunt us.
They live inside us—
And wear our face.

THE WEIGHT OF REMEMBERING

Fool's Anonymous

Hello
My name is Insanity
And I am a fool
It's been 13 hours since I foolishly believed
I had been doing good, keeping a mental distance, not believing the lies
But then, in a moment of weakness and weariness, I slipped
I opened up and let the lies flow in
I soaked them up like the desert devours the rain
I want to do better this time
I will build a bigger wall so that the lies cannot break through
I am standing here now to start anew
I am making a fresh vow to stop being a fool

THE WEIGHT OF REMEMBERING

Cloak and Dagger

Dancing around the dagger that will slice us open if we embrace it
The yearning to reach out and feel the pain is almost too much to bear
Pretending that it isn't there is the only way to keep everything whole and safe
But is safety what we really want
Do we want to let this opportunity to feel pass us by
Should we act like there's not a fire burning on the inside
Go on living life hiding everything, go back to not feeling
Is that even possible
The thing that has been awakened fights for control of my mind
It wants to jump in and see how deep the water is
It takes every ounce of my power to keep it from taking over
But I will keep pushing it down and locking it up
I must if I want to survive unscathed

THE WEIGHT OF REMEMBERING

Too Many Questions

How do I fight the thoughts in my head?
The ones I know are wrong.
Why do I want what I know I can't have?
Is it all in my mind?
Just a figment of my imagination?
Is it all one-sided?
What do I think would happen?
That everything in my mind could happen with
no negative effects?
Am I living in a fantasy of my own creation?
Can I ignore the reality of my own desire?
Pretend like it's not inside me?
Do I want to?

THE WEIGHT OF REMEMBERING

Self-Betrayal

My mind is corrupted
These thoughts aren't my own
Control is betraying me
My willpower is gone

Dimming ever darker
With desire burning bright
It wants to subdue me
But I must continue to fight

Ignore the glance that promises more
The touches that make me burn
Pretend the smiles don't make me melt
That they don't make me yearn

This isn't real
The illusion is just a dream
I tremble with the fear of want
I don't know what's wrong with me

THE WEIGHT OF REMEMBERING

The Battle Within

Oh, the betrayer of my very being
My heart wants what my mind knows it can't have
It cries when the unexpected want is taken away
It bleeds at the loss of the forbidden
It ceases to beat anything but the rhythm of desire
The longing to be heard, touched, known, seen
My mind rejoices at my heart's brokenness
It knows what is right and what is wrong
It does not thrive on unrealistic fantasies
It marches to the rhythm of logic and common sense
It knows how to win the battle raging inside
My heart knows it will lose, but it continues to yearn

THE WEIGHT OF REMEMBERING

Insensible

I looked in his eyes and saw the beauty that I believed was within.

I listened to him speak and heard the regret that was never truly there.

I wrapped myself in his arms and breathed in the lies, transforming them into truth.

I touched his chest and felt the heart that had never really beat for me.

I kissed his lips and tasted the bittersweet hope that I refused to give up.

I surrendered myself and felt the love that was inevitably not.

THE WEIGHT OF REMEMBERING

Unreality

A twisted thought from a twisted mind
A mental breakdown, a reality askew
The left is right, the right is wrong
The day is night, the sun is gone
A walking timebomb, about to explode
A look, a touch, a mistake
A life destroyed; a breath renewed
Alternate universes merging as one
Meeting together in a sweet embrace
Tears shed, lives disrupted, hearts broken
Fix it, push it down, deny it
Fake is real, believe it, embrace it
Ignore it and it will not be
Only the thought, the memory, the unreality

THE WEIGHT OF REMEMBERING

Never Wake Up

Today I dreamt of peace
It was a dream like no other
I was happy
I knew no fear
I had no arguments
No pain
No shame
I held my head up high
Looked forward to the day
The excitement of the unknown
It was a place I never wanted to leave
And then I woke up

THE WEIGHT OF REMEMBERING

Two-Faced

Look in the mirror
Do you even recognize yourself
Do you see the person you show to everyone else
Or do you see the monster lurking within
The one that sees things that are not there
Feels and wants things that cannot be
Have you been so numb for so long that the first bit of affection twists your brain into knots
Get a grip
Stop letting irrational thoughts make you see things that are not there
That *can't* be there

THE WEIGHT OF REMEMBERING

Numb

I was numb inside
My heart was sealed up tight
Then you came along, and I started to feel again
Feel joy, feel hope, feel alive
But why
Why open myself up to the hurt that is sure to come
Why believe in a hopeless situation
Why hope you feel the same
Instead, I will refuse to trust, to live
I will seal my heart up tight
I will be numb inside

THE WEIGHT OF REMEMBERING

City of Lies

I'm a monster living in a land called Delusion
I walk around in a fantasy made completely in my mind
Where things which aren't are
And things that are bad are good
Seeing through a lens of deception that believes wrong can be right
And that black is now white
Where a playful touch is a loving caress
And a look cries out for more
I must beat this monster into submission, obedience, silence
Before it completely destroys me

THE WEIGHT OF REMEMBERING

Addiction

Addiction
Unfathomable Pain
Denial
Never-ending Frustration
Lies
Collateral Damage
Hurt
Unjustifiable Anger
Release
Mistaken Bliss
Confusion
Inescapable Regret
Agony
Empty Promises
Worthless
Forgotten Hope
Torture
Distressed Love
Heartache
Self-inflicted Torment
Death

Hope

I open my mouth to speak the pain that is eating away at my very essence, but no words escape the prison that is my mind.

I don't say that I am dying inside, that I battle a thousand times a day not to give in to the heartache that is destroying me.

I don't ask for someone to help pull me out of the sinking sand that is my despair.

I don't reach out for a hand to hold or a shoulder to cry on when the pits of loneliness beckon me with its sweet release.

I don't talk about how the broken promises and empty words are steadily eroding my hope.

Little by little it is chipping away at my joy, my peace.

No, I don't speak a word.

Instead, I choke on all the things that I cannot say, the unspoken reality.

I smile and say that everything is fine, that I am good.

I dam up the tears that are screaming to be free.

I keep trudging on through the dark tunnel that is suffocating the life inside of me.

I continue walking alone, clinging to the smallest glimmer of hope that things will get better.

I try not to look around at the destruction inside.

I keep my focus on that dim, little light that barely brightens my path.

I keep pushing on.

THE WEIGHT OF REMEMBERING

Buried

Don't imagine
Don't pretend
Come out of the daydream that you're living in
Made up fantasies that are not only fake, but wrong
The unreciprocated yearning that haunts your every step
Close your mind and stop your heart
Don't think
Don't feel
Block out the thoughts that invade
Stop imagining what *is* not and *can*not be
Why do you insist on torturing yourself with the unrealistic desire that you believe has awakened inside of you?
It's not real and neither is what you are feeling
Put it in a box, lock it up tight, and bury it in the deepest depths of your being
Don't try to open it, ever
It can only bring heartache and torment
It isn't real

I'm Sorry

I'm sorry.
Two words that make up both sides of a double-edged sword

One side slices through the pain and heartache of someone wronged
And the other cuts out the beating heart of the one who's heard it too many times

These words can open communication and rebuild bridges that have been broken
But they can also construct a wall so tall and thick that nobody can penetrate it

When whispered with the deepest, most sincere heart, these words can heal
When they are uttered over and over again with no change, they will destroy

I'm sorry are two great words that have amazing power
But there is one thing that they cannot do

They cannot erase a memory
They cannot make you forget what was done or said

I'm sorry can change a mind, but it cannot
change a heart
The pain remains inside, even if the mind has
moved on

We are taught early on to forgive when
someone says those words
But that doesn't mean that we have to trust
them again

How much is too much
Forgiveness is important, but how many times
must you hear, "I'm sorry"

For the hateful words that were spoken
For the actions that showed their love was a lie

How many times is too many to hear and
believe the very overused words
I'm sorry

THE WEIGHT OF REMEMBERING

Too Much to Ask For

She stands at a crossroad in life.
Which way should she go?
What is it that she truly wants?
She searches the furthest-most reaches of her heart.
She knows what it is.
She wants love.
To be seen past her masks.
To be heard in what she's afraid to speak.
To be protected from the monsters in her mind.
She wants to know that she can depend on her love to catch her when she falls.
That he will lift her up when she is down.
That she can lean on him in every part of her life.
That he would never leave her.
Never choose her last.
Never walk away.
Is she asking for too much?
Is she hoping for a fairy tale that could never come true?
Should she just give up hoping that true love exists?
She thinks it does exist, just not for her.

By Any Other Name

"What's in a name?" Shakespeare asked. "That which we call a rose, by any other name, would smell as sweet."

Indeed, he spoke correctly.

If it were called dung, it would still smell as sweet as a rose.

Nothing can change that fact.

To that point, a tiger, by any other name, would still bite, preying on the lives of weaker animals.

A snake, by any other name, would still slither, strangling the life of any who stands in its way.

Why do we, as humans, think this same rule does not apply to us?

Why do we believe that if we love someone enough, they will change?

Have we not learned from the words that Shakespeare has branded on history?

A rose will smell like a rose, no matter what we call it, no matter where it grows, no matter how much we care for it.

When will we take to heart his declaration?

When will we learn that just because someone changes their name, it doesn't change who they are on the inside?

A rose, by any other name, will smell as sweet.

A spider, by any other name, will spin its web.

A frog, by any other name, will leap from this place to that.

A thief, by any other name, will steal.

A cheater, by any other name, will cheat.

A liar, by any other name, will lie.

THE WEIGHT OF REMEMBERING

Battle

I can but I can't
I could but I won't
I would but I shouldn't
I want to but I don't

A battle rages inside
It eats away at me
Do I have the strength to fight it
What if I win
What if it wins

Think
Stay alert
Be ready
Never turn away
Always be on

There's no time to be weak
No time to fall
If I do, who will pick me up
Who will hold me, so I don't fall
Who will take my hand to share their strength

Nobody
I'm alone in this battle
Darkness surrounds me
I can't see anything or anyone
I'm alone

One Coin, Two Faces

"Dig deep, tell me who you are."
How do I tell you the good without noticing the bad?
The confidence without the insecurities?
The rejoices without the heartbreaks?
They are different sides of the same coin.
The side I show is the "good" side.
The side that is full of self-confidence, happiness, hope.
It doesn't doubt in itself.
It is beautiful and happy with itself, despite what others may say or think.
It doesn't care how others treat her.
The wrongs they do to her.
She will overcome them.
The other side, the darker side, sees her differently.
It sees the tears she refuses to shed.
The pain that chips away at the pieces of her broken heart.
It sees her as weak, hopeless, and unimportant.
It whispers lies in her ears that she fights hard not to believe.
It tells her that she isn't pretty, she isn't strong, she isn't worthy.
That she will never be loved.
That side doesn't get to see the light of day very often.
She's afraid that if it does, it will destroy her.

That she will never find happiness and joy.
No, the other side has to be contained.
Kept under lock and key.
It doesn't get to show itself.
The only time it breaks through is when it has been so packed down so tight that the pressure is too strong.
It busts through the seams of its prison.
But even then, it can only be seen for a brief moment.
A blinking of an eye.
If one isn't paying attention, they'll miss it.
They will only see the side that knows she believes she is enough.
She is strong and confident and doesn't need to depend on anyone.
Sometimes her strength is also her weakness though.
She stays so strong that she builds up walls to keep anyone from getting too close, lest they see the dark side and run away.
She stays diligent.
She can't let the other side out.
Ever.
It might overtake her, then who would she be?

THE WEIGHT OF REMEMBERING

Too Broken

Second rate
Second thought
Second choice
Why do I always get left behind
Why is it I am never the first choice
Why do I keep letting it happen
Never smart enough
Never pretty enough
Never good enough
When will someone accept me for me
When do I get to be the one, the only one
When do I get to be loved
Too often abandoned
Too often betrayed
Too often destroyed
What do I do with the shattered pieces of my heart
What happens if I can't put them back together
What if it's too late to

THE WEIGHT OF REMEMBERING

Strangers

I looked into the eyes of a stranger today

I smiled and said hello

Asked how her day was

She smiled back and said it was great

But when I looked deeper, I could see she wasn't telling the truth

Her eyes were full of sorrow, anguish almost

I stepped closer and asked how she was really doing

Again, she just smiled and said she was great

We stood staring at each other, not speaking

But as I looked, I watched the story of her life start to unfold

I could see the scars like open wounds that she tried to cover

The doubt she carried in the very core of her

I could see that she had never known true love

That she almost didn't believe it was real

I glimpsed a heart so broken she didn't think it could ever be put together again

I felt her despair of ever believing she was enough to keep

For someone to love and cherish her like they do in fairytales

I could hear the screams she fought every day to silence

The ones that were yearning to break free

I wanted to reach out to hold her

To tell her that she wasn't alone

But I didn't think it would do any good

I could tell that she was the kind of person who had been broken so much that she wouldn't believe it

We just watched each other, listening to what words could not say

Her eyes started to brim with all the emotions she kept bottled up

I wanted to tell her to just let them fall

That she might feel better if she did

I started to drown in the tears that were diligently trying to escape her eyes

Before I could say a word, she smiled, blinked back the tears, and walked away from the mirror

THE WEIGHT OF REMEMBERING

Monstrous Desires

What do you do when you want what you cannot have?
And what you have is destroying you inside?
When you read too much into every word, every gesture, every touch?
When it leaves you longing for more, yet at the same time disgusted with yourself?
How can you think like that?
How can you feel what you've made up in your mind?
You should know better.
You should be stronger.
You are a monster.
But that's what it is.
A monster lurking inside of me, fighting for control.
Using its every breath to break my barriers.
To get me to do the unthinkable.
To forsake all wisdom and morals.
To jump off the edge of what is right and just live in the moment.
To embrace the unknown.
I will fight that monster with all I have, even when it's not what I want.
I must fight, and I must win.
Anything else is madness.

New Normal

Please, can you help me?
I'm being held captive.
I wish I could say it's against my will, but it's not.
And yet, I can't escape.
How did I get here?
Well, it's a tale as old as time.
My captor didn't seem like a captor at first.
He was sweet and loving, attentive to everything I would want or need.
He overfed me with all the love I could ingest.
Not that I was complaining about being fed so much love.
I basked in it, flourished even.
But as time went on, he fed me less and less.
I started to lose the luster in my eyes upon seeing him.
Sometimes even dreaded that he was there.
I could feel myself slipping further and further away.
Slowly fading into someone I didn't recognize.
But then he'd feed me again, and I would adore him again.
This cycle went on over and over and over.
My body became accustomed to receiving those little chunks of love.

So much so, that I didn't see that I was wasting away to nothing.
Becoming just an empty shell to be filled up and emptied at his whimsy.
And now, I'm stuck.
I can't escape.
I'm afraid that I will be in this place forever.
Living just to be fed little nuggets of love.
Not a healthy diet of it, but just enough to keep me from dying.
Honestly, sometimes I think that would be a blessing.
Not physically dying, but killing that emotional beast inside that craves to be held, to be loved, to be accepted.
It's her fault that I'm stuck.
That I can't escape.
She thrives on whatever love nuggets she can get, even if they are unhealthy.
She looks for love everywhere and in everything.
What she doesn't see is that what she's accepting as nourishment, is slowly poisoning me.
It's tearing away the very essence of who I am, who I want to be, how I want to live, how I want to be loved.
I'm starting to think it's normal.

That just barely living is living enough.
I can see my little girl's dream of a "happily-ever-after" drifting away.
The one that saw love as something that could conquer all.
A girl who dreamed of being someone's everything.
That someone would love her just as she was and that she would be enough to keep him by her side forever.
That she would never have to beg to be fed his love.
He would give it freely and openly, and only to her.
But her dreams are becoming nightmares.
They're being replaced with a "this is all you're worthy of" mentality.
She could have more, but she's not worthy enough for it.
She should just be quiet and accept whatever love nuggets she can get fed.
That she doesn't need a well-rounded diet to survive.
Eating here and there is enough.
And if she has to swallow the poison of neglect to get fed more love, then that's ok.
She's getting what she is worthy enough to get.
It's what she deserves in this life.

I'm learning to accept that this is just my lot in life.
That it is normal and I shouldn't expect anything more.
At least I'm getting fed occasionally, right?
I wish I could have more.
I wish you could help me escape this prison of "it is what it is."
Believing that nothing is going to change.
That this is the lot in life I deserve.
But I need to face reality.
You can't help me.
No one can.
I'm stuck.

THE WEIGHT OF REMEMBERING

Good Enough

You're healing
You feel better
You're not hurt by choices you didn't make
You refuse to be again
And you think it's really true
But then someone says something, and it feels like you've been sucker-punched
You're faced with the reality that, yet again, you weren't enough
Pretty enough, loving enough
You weren't good enough to keep them from straying
That no matter how much you gave of yourself, they always chose someone else
You remember how you tried to conform to what they needed you to be
You encouraged them and loved them
Tried to be everything they asked
But they still didn't want you to be their one and only
You weren't what they wanted
You weren't good enough for them
You aren't good enough for anyone

A Show

Smile
Put on a show
Don't let them see how broken you really are
You can't
You have to be strong
Be everything to everyone
Do what you have to do
Swallow the tears
The pain
The shame
Act like everything is great
Make them believe it
Make yourself believe it
Show no weakness
If you do, they will break you
Take advantage
Make fun
You can't let them know
Nobody can know
You're weak
Pathetic
Don't cry
Muscle through it
Pack it away
Don't think

Don't remember
Don't feel
Fake it 'til you make it
No screaming
No reactions
No pain
Only joy
Only peace
Only laughter
Forget how you really feel
Imagine it's not there
Not real
Not destroying you
Pretend
If you start to fall apart
Smile

THE WEIGHT OF REMEMBERING

Wait

One happy day, hands and hearts joined
Tears of joy fell, a new life begun
Many years passed, full of lies and deceit
Now broken hearted, a love undone

Tell me what happened, please tell me the way
How a once happy person now struggles each day
I try to be strong, and I try to hold tight
To the promise from God that He'll make things alright

But each passing day is harder than the last
Is it now time to put the present in the past
Or should I keep walking, holding tight to His hand
Let Him lead me through stormy seas and onto dry land

Sometimes it seems that I'll never be free
To be happy in love with the one who chose me
I'll have to keep walking and try to stay in His will
Until the promise He made has been finally fulfilled

THE WEIGHT OF REMEMBERING

Remember

Broken, shattered, destroyed
At least once a day I die
My heart stops beating
The breath freezes in my lungs
Most thoughts cease to exist
And I remember

The pain, the sorrow, the shame
A life that was promised, then torn apart
A love that was given, then thrown away
Little by little my breath returns
My heart starts beating again
Because I remember

My worth, my strength, my resilience
A life that is not over, even if a love is
A heart that, though pieced back together, is
stronger than before
I take a step towards my healing
Start to believe that I deserve better
I will continue to remember

I'm Great

"How are you doing today?"
Before I answer, I check myself
I make sure my smile is firmly in place
Ensure there is a sparkle in my eyes
I use my vibrant, peppy voice
"I'm great!"
I give a nod to make sure they really believe it
But the truth is, I'm not
I'm not great
I'm not even good
I'm barely hanging on to ok
Tears are hiding just behind the surface
Ready to hijack my continence at a moment's weakness
Threatening to shout their truth to anyone
who dares to see beyond the words
Who pushes to past the walls I erect
These walls are not to keep people out
But to hold me up
To keep me from falling apart
Those who choose to scale those walls should beware
This pain is not for the faint of heart
It's the kind of pain that, if it's let loosed,
would utterly destroy everything and everyone it touches

It is impossible to tame, to tamp down, to control
It tears away at your soul, your very being
It's a flesh-eating bacterium that can't be stopped
It lays waste to any and all hope
This pain must not be released
I must lock it away
Not let it be free to beat me down
So, when people ask how I am, I will continue to smile, nod, and joyfully say
"I am great."

THE WEIGHT OF REMEMBERING

Relentless Heart

Why do you torment me so?
Why do you insist on clinging to a hope that
has been blown away on the breeze of
betrayal time and time again?
Trick me into letting down my meticulously
placed and fortified walls?
Is it not enough that I have tasted the bitter
pill of a love become a lie?
Have these eyes not overflowed the ocean?
My heart is become encased in a solid ball of
ice.
The frigid kiss of shattered trust adding yet
another frozen layer.
Then you come and begin to melt its
protective layer with the whispered promises
that are never kept.
But oh, my foolish heart.
It leaps for joy at the declaration of rebuilding
the broken road.
It wants to start forging another bond.
It is a relentless taskmaster.
It fights me every day for control.

THE WEIGHT OF REMEMBERING

The Monster Inside

There is a monster living inside of me
A monster that will not die, no matter how hard I try to destroy it
It leaches on and sucks away all of my strength
I push it down and lock it away over and over again
But the moment I think I'm safe, it breaks out
Grows in determination
Overtakes my sanity
Hides reason behind its delusions of happily ever after
I will push it down again
But I'm afraid that it will only come back stronger than ever
Tricking me into complacency
Again

Still She Sits

I see her sitting there all alone
And I wonder if she knows how sad she looks
So undeniably hopeless
I watch her get chosen second over and over again
How she gets used and abused time after time
Yet she continues to put on rose colored glasses
Horse blinders
She refuses to let go of the delusion that someone will put her first
That they will see her as a girl worth fighting for
Worth dying for
She believes their lies when they say she's perfect
They wouldn't do anything to lose her
They love her
I want to scream at her to wake up
But that won't do any good
I have to just stand here with her
Try my best fend off the pain and heartache that will inevitably come
Slowly try to get her to see that hoping the wolves won't eat her alive is futile

A wild beast is a wild beast
It doesn't change because you want it to
And a man who has shown her his true
colors aren't a beautiful rainbow
He is just someone who knows what to say
to make her feel better
Words to make her hang on to an imaginary
future
All the while she sits there all alone
Still hoping against hope that this will be the
one

Masked Woman

I'm not alright
But I can't say so
I have to be strong, unbreakable
Put on a mask so that nobody sees the scars
The open wounds that fester, eating away at
my flesh
My insides churn, twisting me into a knot
But I stand up straight
Pretend like I'm ok, despite the destructive
thoughts that consume me
Burn me up inside
The world will see the strong, put-together
woman I need to be to live another day
But I still see the woman who is frozen
The one who dares not let the pain sink in
lest she fall and never get back up

Bleeding Hands

I lift my arms and try to move things in my life
But I can't seem to get them work right
They aren't doing what I want them to do
I look to see what the problem is
It's not my arms, they're working just fine
It's my hands
Whenever I try to use them, they refuse to operate
They are too broken
Bleeding too much
I don't remember hurting them on anything
But when I try to pick something up, it slips back out
My hands are too slick with the blood that seems to never stop
I look around to see what could have sliced hands open, but I see nothing
Then I remember
It's my heart's fault
Every time it lets someone close and they break it, I have to pick the pieces back up
Sliver by sliver
Sharper than a razor blade
I've had to pick them up and put them back together so many times

The shards have started to cut through to the bones
My hands have become unrecognizable
Unusable
If my heart breaks again, I won't be able to pick the pieces up
Won't be able to put it back together again
My hands won't let
They can't
They don't work anymore

THE WEIGHT OF REMEMBERING

Ghost of a Life Past

I'm here but, but I'm not
I can see what's going on around me
Hear the conversations
Even join in at times
I smile at the appropriate moments
Respond to comments made my way
To all appearances, everything's fine
I am my normal self
But if they could see inside, they'd see the truth
That a ghost has taken up residency
It's not me smiling out at them
I have been relegated to the furthest reaches of my mind
The pain and heartache I had buried has come to claim its own land
It has taken over
When you look at me, you don't see me
You can't, I am no longer living
You only see the ghost of who I used to be

Always the Fool

Why do I cling to hope like breath to fill my lungs?
Blood to make my heart beat?
I have been shown what a lion looks like, yet I continue to call it a kitten.
It's claws not big nor strong enough to hurt me.
I ignore the gashes that have been ripped from my skin time and time again.
Pretend they're not there, they don't exists, never happened.
That the lion can be tamed, be sweet and cuddly.
That it would never hurt me.
That it would ignore its basic instincts because of its deep love for me.
But again and again I am deceived.
I allow myself to get too close to its soft fur, drawn in by its gentle purr.
It brings me close, warms me.
Then when I let my guard down enough to relax, it strikes.
Sinks its teeth in deep and rips out my heart.
Shreds every ounce of my being.
Leaves me to stitch the pieces that remain

back together.
I heal and get drawn back in.
Hope fills my lungs.
And I start the process all over again.

Façade

Clear skies
A field of beautiful wildflowers
A calm, shimmering lake
Birds flying peacefully in the distance
Maybe a blanket laid out, ready to enjoy a home-packed lunch
Fruit freshly picked just for you
Perhaps some soft, romantic music playing softly in the background
A slow dance under a fairytale moon
The perfect day
This is what I imagine people think is in my mind when I face them with a smile
But they only see the dream of what I wish it was like
In reality
There are no flowers or gently rolling fields
In fact, there is no land to be seen
There are no birds
The storm is too strong for them to fly in
The skies are 20 shades of black
The only light is from the bults of electricity that strike so close, my skin starts to singe
But before it can catch fire, the storm tossed waves rise up to dowse the would-be flames
They knock me down
Forces their way into my lungs

Chokes me
I don't lose consciousness though
The winds that keep the birds from flying
enters and shoves the water back out
I stand on shaky legs to see if the end is near
But there is nothing but this eternal night
The endless cycle of stand, get knocked
down, stand again, get pushed back down
This sea is tumultuous
The storm overpowering
But I can't turn around
I have to make my way through it if I ever
expect to make it out alive
To see what awaits on the other side
To become whole
To find myself

Hold On

Just like the titanic after it hit the iceberg,
I can feel myself sinking beneath the cold,
murky waters of my emptiness.
I get tossed a lifesaver, only to see the rope get cut.
I am left grasping this little respite of hope that barely keeps my head above the surface.
Ships come near to help, but don't get close enough to see
that I'm not just taking a casual swim.
I am fighting against the ever-growing current that is trying to destroy me.
It taunts me.
It pushes me close to the shore, allows me to find my footing,
then sends a towering wave to knock me down and suck me back in.
I want to be rescued, but I fear I may succumb to this monster inside.
This entity that wishes for nothing more than to devour my joy, my peace, my happiness, my hope, my very soul.
I will keep swimming, even as my arms tremble with fatigue.
I must not give in to the pain of the past,

the sorrow of loneliness,
the emptiness of words forgotten,
the anger of broken promises,
the bitterness that wages war against my mind.
Even as my fingers cramp with the pain of holding on,
I must keep a firm grip on the only thing keeping my head above this ocean of despair,
this small ring of faith.
I must not release my hold on my lifesaver.

THE WEIGHT OF REMEMBERING

IF I WAKE TOMORROW

*Stillness doesn't mean giving up.
Some days, survival sounds like,
"Maybe I'll try again… tomorrow."*

A Pheonix Rising

I thought about you today
About what life would look like if you weren't with me
And I didn't shed a tear

I sit here trying to reason it out
Why wouldn't the tears come if a love was ending
But my eyes stayed dry

Are my tears protesting
Perhaps refusing to fall yet again for one who has hurt me
Who didn't think I was enough

Or maybe they're gone
Maybe they were all used up by past promises and betrayals
The ones that weren't supposed to happen... again

Are my tears the problem
Or is it a heart that no longer beats at the thought of you
A mind that has gone numb

I used to think I'd die
That life would end if we weren't together anymore
Then I realized I was already dead

Promise upon promise and lie upon lie
My life ended a little more with each broken declaration
Until I was just a shell

A picture of who I was
Before I let you in time and time again with frivolous words of love
A picture torn to shreds

Now a new person is here
A phoenix who was raised up from the ashes of a love set ablaze
A phoenix with no more tears

THE WEIGHT OF REMEMBERING

The Little Things

I want to feel the tender embrace of love
I want to know that I am enough
That someone chooses me for me
I want a hand to pull me close
I want to be held, tucked away from the world
So close that two hearts beat as one
I want to be heard, not just listened to
I want to be seen in the deepest parts I hide
To be understood when no words are spoken
I want someone to carry me through my pain
I want to know that I can be weak
That someone will hold me if/when I break
I want a hug that speaks louder than words
I want a kiss that melts the coldest heart
A soft yet passionate sharing of souls

Her Decision

How did she get to this unhappy place
She asked herself everyday
Would this be her lot in life forever
Was this the only way

She tried to smile through the pain
Act like nothing was ever wrong
She'd only ever wanted to be loved
To know that she belonged

Then she faced her greatest hurdle
The hardest one of her life
Choose to live the way she's always lived
Filled with heartbreak and strife

Hiding the tears and ignoring the anguish
Of being lied to yet again
Or acknowledge the pain that she'd hidden away
Refusing to bury it again

She pondered the question both day and night
Deciding which path to take
Choose a new way of life that is scary to try
Or keep living a life that is fake

When she finally determined what step she should take
She was afraid to make a move
But if she ever wanted to be happy in this life
It was something she'd had to do

So she left the road of least resistance
To forge a brand-new trail
Where this path of life would take her
Only time would tell

She left the fears and doubts behind
Embracing her new-found self
Leaving behind the heartache and betrayal
She chose to love herself

THE WEIGHT OF REMEMBERING

Growing Pains

She chose to love herself
But does she really know what that means
How does she change how she's always lived
How does she change her dreams

She's given of herself for so long
That she doesn't know what it's like to receive
She handed over her heart so full of hope
Only for it to be deceived

She smiled when she was dying inside
Burying the doubt and pain
She hated feeling sad and angry
So she pretended and put on a smile yet again

Years and years of wearing her mask
Ignoring what was happening inside
Has caused her to forget who she was
She only knows how to hide

Hide what she's thinking, feelings ignored
Pretending they aren't there, aren't real
Living life in this shadowed world
Was the only way she's learned to deal

Fake it 'til she made it, ignore the ugly truth
Was the motto of her life
Now she struggles to know what feelings are real
And which ones are simply lies

Can she find who she is and wants to be
Without the bondage of fear holding her down
Can she swim against the tide of her normal
Or will the buried truths make her drown

Can she open the chest that holds all her secrets
And examine them one by one
Can she see the truths of her painful past
And do what needs to be done

Can she learn to live in the great wide open
Free of fear and shame
Can she face the demons that plague her thoughts
The ones she's tried to cast away

Can she start anew when her heart was shattered again
Without bottling the pain and sorrow

Can she be truthful with herself about how she feels
Can she see a better tomorrow

Can she see the facts for what they are
Can she believe that there is more
Can she stay and hope she won't get hurt again
Can she believe this love is worth fighting for

Can she look in the mirror and see past the mask
Can she step into the unknown
Can she risk bearing her heart and soul
Can she reap the seeds that have been sown

Can she find the hurts she's locked tight away
Can she call them out by name
Can she give each one its own space to be heard
Can she survive these growing pains

THE WEIGHT OF REMEMBERING

This Day

This day, if only for today, she is choosing to live
Live for the life she didn't see before
The life she never knew she needed
Where she is strong, and beautiful, and confident
Where she can trust in herself, and that she is enough
More than enough
She doesn't doubt that she is worthy of love
A love that is pure, and true, and faithful
A love that never leaves
That chooses her, without fail
She chooses to believe in her own self-worth
Refuses to fall prey to the lies that circle around her mind
The lies that tell her that she is less than
Today, this day, if only for today, she is choosing her

Once Upon a Lie

Once upon a time
There was a love worth fighting for
A never-ending love
It was cherished and adored

The prince valued his princess
As a treasure greater than gold
He promised her a future
Where together they'd grow old

She trusted this prince
With everything she held dear
She gave him her whole heart
With all its hopes and dreams and fears

Never in a billion years
Did she expect their love would die
Until she woke up one day
To find that the prince had lied

His words said he wanted her
That she was all he truly desired
But his actions told a different story
That set their love on fire

Destroyed the hope she had
That he would ever choose her first
Made her almost believe
That she would be forever cursed

That nobody she loved
Would ever think she was enough
She would forever be the one
Whose love was always rebuffed

Until the day she began to see
That she didn't need him anymore
She didn't need anyone else
To fight her battle or to win her war

She only needed to look inside
To find her value and trust her worth
No, she didn't need a protector
She found that she could fight for her

Unexpected

Sometimes someone enters your life when you aren't expecting it.
You believed that life was what it was and you just smiled through it.
Then this person opens your eyes to things You'd thought were beyond your reach.
Things that were gone for so long, you gave up on them.
Things that you didn't even realize you were missing.
Or if you did, you just ignored them because what was the point?
But they showed you a different life.
They showed you that it was ok to want more, expect more.
That you were someone worth loving.
Someone who deserved more.
They never said a word, but you saw it through them anyway.
This person may only be with you for a moment in time, but that moment will last a lifetime.
You will never forget what they did for you, without them even trying.

You grew into a stronger you than you never knew you could be.
You started to believe in things you'd given up on long ago.
All because this person entered your life when you weren't expecting it.

THE WEIGHT OF REMEMBERING

Just for a Moment

I want to give up, surrender
Not because I'm ready to trust again
But because it feels easier to let it go than to keep my boundaries up
To be strong all on my own
Because truth is, I want to be held
To be wrapped in an embrace so tight that my worries melt away
Where I can feel cared for, loved, wanted
Where, for just a moment, I can let go of the pain
I can have someone share the burden of my heart
I want to give up, but I won't
I have to be strong, even if I feel alone
Even if I long for arms to hold me
For a voice to whisper in my ear that it'll be ok
For someone to hold me up for a little while so I can rest

AUTHOR'S NOTE

*If you saw yourself in these pages,
you're not alone.*

*I wrote this for the nights you couldn't sleep,
for the days you couldn't speak,
and for the moments when all you could do was
hold back the tears.*

*This book is for the ones who've loved too hard,
broken too many times,
and never quite knew how to put the ache into
words.*

*I hope somewhere between the silence and the
sorrow,
you felt seen.*

—Makenzie Rae,
*giving voice to the silent truths that suffocated
our hope.*

www.ingramcontent.com/pod-product-compliance
Lightning Source LLC
Chambersburg PA
CBHW031639040426
42453CB00006B/146